CRUSH SCHOOL 2

10 Study Secrets Every High Schooler Should Know

oskar cymerman

Focus 2 Achieve | focus2achieve.com

FOCUS 2 ACHIEVE
Published by *Orange Dog Creations*,
a Focus 2 Achieve company
www.focus2achieve.com
Minneapolis, MN
USA

First published in digital format by Focus 2 Achieve.

ABOUT THE AUTHOR

Oskar Cymerman is a teacher, writer, and a small educational consulting and products business owner. He is passionate about how the human brain learns best, personal improvement, and professional growth. He blogs at *focus2achieve.com/blog* and for the Bam Radio Network. His new podcast will launch on the Bam Radio Network in September, 2017.

Oskar's main interests revolve around understanding how the human brain acquires, processes, and remembers information. He uses this understanding to teach students and train teachers and other professionals.

Oskar's favorite clients are academic organizations and innovative forward-thinking organizations in need of professional development on teaching, learning, and leading in the 21st century. For workshop inquiries, call 651.757.6635 or email *oskar@focus2achieve.com*.

Crush School 2: 10 Study Secrets Every High Schooler Should Know is Oskar's third book.

He is currently working on 2 more books (maybe 3, who knows?); one on 21st century teaching and learning; and another on effective use of smartphones for teachers and students. Sign up for his free newsletter for updates and to receive articles and infographics on life, living, and learning.

focus2achieve.com
Twitter: *@focus2achieve*

ALSO BY OSKAR CYMERMAN

Crush School: Every Student's Guide To Killing It In The Classroom.

The Power of Three: Simplify to Amplify.

Check out educational products in Oskar's Amazon store: www.amazon.com/shops/f2a

TABLE OF CONTENTS

Schools are dead...

... but learning isn't.

I wrote my first book, _Crush School: Every Student's Guide To Killing It In The Classroom_ after realizing that most interesting education books are written for adults, and the ones students are forced to use in class mostly suck.

They're not just uninteresting. They are dull and written in some weird code no one can, or wants to understand. And, they make your backpack look like you're about to set off on a two week long hike in the wilderness, which would be cool if you're into that sort of thing, except for the fact that you're surrounded by concrete, glass, and steel. You're not a horse either, so what's the deal? I mean really...

And here's one more unpopular opinion coming from this teacher. Most of the stuff in those books is useless. Most of the so-called knowledge can be googled. Some of this information will be outdated before you hit work. A lot of it is irrelevant right now.

The simple truth many schools don't want to accept, is that teaching subjects and giving tests is the wrong way to go about education. This is why many students hate school, but actually love learning. Think about it. School might not be your thing, but you surely have hobbies, passions, and other things you choose to learn. No one tells you to learn them. You just do, because you want to. They matter and are worth your time. Why can't we do more of that at school?

But here's the kicker. The stuff school books are made of is not all bad. The problem is that you're not using most of what you're learning in meaningful ways. There's often no connection to your life. So, school sucks. But you must get through it.

Let's talk chemistry. Why do many schools require all students take chemistry to graduate? It's not like everyone will be a chemist when they grow up. In chemistry, you learn stoichiometry to calculate the amounts of chemicals made in chemical reactions. Even if you do a related experiment, the product is some white powder you can't eat, sniff, or smoke. You made it for no real reason. What's the point?

But what if that powder was used for something? What if you could take some of that stuff home and wash a stain out of that one shirt you spilled Kool Aid on? Now, you made something relevant. The abstract concepts became a real thing. Isn't that cool? Unfortunately, this almost never happens in school.

But this is precisely why you need to learn how to learn; how to figure things out on your own, based on what you need. If you have the right skills, you can figure out how to make soap or meth, build a website or a car, or code the next Snapchat or Pokemon GO. Even if you're not interested in any of the things just mentioned, wouldn't it be cool to know that you could if you wanted to?

That's what this book is about; gaining the skills and the confidence that will help you say *I can do it*, no matter what *it* is. This is what the future will require. Actually, that's wrong. The future is now.

So... If school sucks for you, let it be dead to you. Just focus on learning, because you will need mad skills to survive in the urban jungle that awaits when you're out. Learn how to learn, and do it the smart way, so you can constantly improve yourself. If you know how to learn, you'll be able to reinvent yourself and start over when things don't work out.

And if things do work out? You'll know why they did. Besides, things can always get better. If you don't improve them, someone else will. Count on that, but always bet on yourself.

HOW TO USE WHAT YOU LEARN

This book is uber short. The main reason is that I wanted you to know you don't have to read a 700-page tome to become good at learning. I wanted you to feel the information is easy to access. I wanted you to be able to put this small book in your backpack or purse and carry with you to refer to whenever you need to.

It'll come in handy.

Learning is about strategy; the "know how" of how your brain processes information best and how to use it most effectively. Understanding how meaning is made in your brain and how memory works, will help you improve academically, regardless of how much you suck or rock at school. If you find yourself struggling with a concept or subject, open this book and try a new way of doing it. Even if you're good at school, you'll find things you didn't know. They will help you get even better.

But don't just read this book. Read it actively. Help your mind process the information right away. The best way to do this is to underline information you want to remember or use, and take notes explaining it in the white spaces. Rewriting concepts in your own words helps you remember and understand. It makes them yours. But that's not enough. You must also use what you learn.

Knowledge is not power. If you have it, but don't use it, it's useless. Knowledge is the potential you must realize by application. This is how you get skills. When you learn a concept and use it to create something, it sticks. If you practice it repeatedly, it becomes a skill. Much like a great basketball player never stops practicing his jump shot, you can become awesome at learning by using tried and true strategies over and over.

For example, if you keep underlining important passages in books and paraphrasing them in the margins, it'll become a skill that helps you get meaning out of what you read for life. All you have to do is keep at it. Do it each time you read. It'll also make learning more enjoyable and easier.

Speaking of easier... I designed *Crush School 2* to be easier; to help you remember what you read better. Each chapter consists of 3 parts.

What you'll learn is a quick intro to the chapter. It gets you thinking about things you do or don't do when you learn. It also introduces what you're about to read.

Chapter (Chapter name here) section is used to explain the actual learning secret, why it works for your brain, and how to do it. It also gives many examples of how you can apply it.

Each chapter also includes a hack, a different way of studying for you to look at and use. It might be a quick tip or an action plan. Whatever it is, it will help you level up your learning. As an example, here's the r*ead actively hack* mentioned before:

1. Underline or highlight information you find useful, so you can review it quickly any time you are studying.
2. Take notes in white spaces (margins etc.), paraphrasing what you're learning or how you could use it to learn better.

Chapter Summary is a quick paragraph that serves as a reminder of the key points. Do not skip it, or the **What you'll learn** part, because if you do, you won't remember as well. If you don't remember, you can't use it. If you don't use it, why are you reading it? Read actively!

For more study aides, check out my free learning visuals at
focus2achieve.com/products.

Chapter 1: Sleep

What you'll learn

This has been preached to you all your life by your parental units, but do you know what happens in your brain when you don't sleep enough? Read on to find out. You'll also learn how much sleep you need and a couple sleep hacks to help you learn better.

Sleep

The human brain uses 20 percent of the body's energy.

So?, you might say, and you'd be right except for the toxins.

Toxins? If you think that's gross, you're right. When your brain uses that 20 percent, it produces these nasty metabolic toxins. The good news is, the brain fluid washes these toxins away when you sleep. The bad news is, when you don't sleep long enough, the toxins stick around.

Do you remember a time (like yesterday maybe?) when you woke up kind of foggy and out of it, because you stayed up too late and got up too early? Your mind was clouded, which made it hard to focus. It might have taken you awhile to register what your mom, dad, or sister wanted from you right then and there. All because of the toxins in your brain. You didn't give your brain enough time to relax and use the brain fluid to flush them out.

Skipping on some sleep once might seem like no big deal, but there are studies that prove lack of sleep slows down processing and makes learning new stuff more difficult. Even one night!

Why is that?, might you ask.

Toxins kill brain cells; these neurons you own, right beneath your hairstyle. If you're thinking *Who cares, I have like billions of them*, you might be right. If you're lucky, the brain cells that miraculously stored that lame joke you heard someone tell yesterday in the hallway between English and Math, will be destroyed. But what if you're wrong? What if the neurons you really need to do well on that history test get killed off? You just never know...

And there's more. Lack of sleep adds up. One night might or might not matter too much, but keep doing it and you'll be like Beavis and Butthead. They didn't do so well in school. Not even gym.

So do everything you can to get 9 hours of sleep and this is on the low end. I don't know you, but I'm pretty sure you most likely need 10 or 11.

And take a nap when you can after studying. Or study right before you go to bed. You might dream about this stuff and your brain will make new connections. These little hacks will help you with understanding and remembering new information.

Chapter Summary

The brain produces toxins. It cleans them out when you sleep. Except when you don't... Then, the toxins stay and impair your brain. That's bad for thinking, understanding, and learning. You most likely need 10-11 hours of sleep each night. The real tragedy happens when you don't sleep. The 9 more tips you're about to get become less effective or totally useless. But don't take my word for it. Just promise me you'll sleep on it.

Get sleep you always must. - Yoda

Chapter 2: Move

What you'll learn

I know of at least one book written specifically on this topic, but I'll try to give you what I know in 3 pages. You will learn why movement helps learning and what you can do at home and school to use it for your becoming a better student benefit.

Move

In case you haven't noticed, this book talks about the brain a lot. But then, this here chapter is about movement. And since it's not good to move your brain, because concussions really suck, let's talk about moving your feet and other parts and how that helps your brain, which helps your thinking, which helps your learning.

The story begins with Sir Craven Caveman craving a meal. He ate everything there was to eat around his cave and found himself starving. He wasn't that smart at the time, but by sheer luck, or more likely thanks to a powerful survival instinct, he realized he had two options. One, die. Two, move and find food or die trying.

Both options had a high risk of death associated with them, but the second option at least promised a few thrills and possibly offered survival. Lucky for you and I, Sir Caveman ventured out, undoubtedly collected a few bruises along the way, and walked, ran, and climbed his way to survival.

I know. You're probably like *What does some dumb cave dweller turned wanderer have to do with me? I can get my fried chicken, nanas, and coconuts at the store!*

You're right, but... When Sir Caveman left his comfy cave and started hustling in the hood, his brain became bigger.

He was discovering new surroundings, dealing with which required more brain power. He encountered entirely new things. He had to make sense out of them to decide whether he can use them, or if he should run from them. The deadly things were bigger, stronger, and faster than him. To survive, Sir Caveman had to be smarter.

Each day, he was running, climbing, and jumping to avoid, protect, gather, and kill. He was learning how to survive, and ultimately thrive, in new, changing, and hostile environments. He was doing it all while moving a lot.

As Sir Caveman was moving around, his heart was pumping more blood, which delivered more oxygen to his soon to be bigger brain. Dealing with the challenges of the changing environment required increased processing power. In addition to evolving a bigger brain and more brain neurons, new neural connections were being made in Sir Caveman's brain. The continuous wandering around led to strengthening of the existing and formation of new connections, as he used past experiences to respond to new situations. Sir Caveman got a lot smarter by moving and while moving. He learned to learn and he learned a lot. End of story.

Except, it's just the beginning for you. Sir Craven Caveman's story is proof that vegging out on the couch, or sitting at a desk for prolonged periods of time, is a bad way to learn. To get smarter faster, get moving and keep moving!

Exercise if you can. If you can't or hate it, get moving in other ways. If you're in a dogless house, walk your cat, who cares? Otherwise, walk the dog. Do stretches. Get a standing desk. Bike to a friend's house or school. No elevators or escalators. Climb.

The point is not to work up a sweat, but to get more oxygen to your brain. To increase your processing power. To make and strengthen more neural connections. To make learning easier and more enjoyable. To make you smarter. Most teachers won't tell you that learning while moving is the most natural way to learn. They might be afraid of losing control or simply don't know. Now you know.

The tough thing is... There are teachers who want you to stay seated for the full hour of class. That sucks! So, what are you gonna do about it?

Challenging them in front of other students, or using the tale of Sir Caveman to shine the light on the situation, is not the answer. But... Can you talk to them in private and ask if it'd be okay to stand up and stretch every now and then? Would they be willing to let you have a 3 minute water fountain break if you explained how it helps you learn? Can your parents intervene if the teacher is a stiff immovable object? The key is to have the know how and to be proactive. So for the love of learning, do something! Act.

As for the hacks I promised you... When tired, or stuck on something, or stuck and tired, stand up. Move and maybe the fresh shot of oxygen in the new blood will be the magic needed to snap out of it. It might cause a spark; a sudden flash of genius, who knows? It happens all the time! Besides, the human brain gets tired super fast and needs breaks. You'll be more productive and creative when you mix focused work with movement breaks.

Chapter Summary

Movement increases oxygen to the brain which helps you learn. How can you add more movement to life and school? Do it.

Fall if you will, but move you must. - Yoda

Chapter 3: Be Specific

What you'll learn

*Do you procrastinate? What if I showed you a way to trick your brain into **not** putting things off?* It's all about simplifying learning by being specific about it. Oh, and planning stuff... It's easy.

Be Specific

Imagine this: You have a big math test coming up and don't know where to begin your studying. What do you do?

Thinking *Study for the math test,* may be too hard for your brain to handle. The more stuff your brain has to hold and process, the more overwhelmed it gets. It can comfortably deal with maybe 3 things at a time, but if the test requires learning say 7 big topics, your brain begins experiencing "the pain". The pain leads to procrastination. Procrastination protects you from more pain (at least temporarily) and information overload. After all, your brain's number one job is to help you survive whatever jungle you find yourself in.

But there's a better way...

The answer is simple.

To get ready for the upcoming test and to avoid procrastination, you have to simplify. The best way to do this is to have specific goals for your test preparation, to make a plan of study, and follow it. Let me show you how to make DA PLAN. It'll rock your school world.

What are you waiting for? Flip the page!

DA PLAN

1. **Write down the big topics.** If you're not sure what they are exactly, approach your teacher with pen and paper in hand, and instead of asking *What should I study for the test?*, ask *What are the major concepts and problems I need to know for the test?* See? You're more specific already!

2. **Study 1 to 3 big topics at a time.** Specify the supporting information for each big topic and focus on mastering it. Try to explain these ideas to yourself or someone else.

3. **Mix it up** (See Chapter 6 Practice Smart). Basically, once you studied the concepts separately for a while, it's good to jump around between them.

Now for your regularly scheduled learning hack...

If it's a single concept or two you're learning, you can specify it by saying exactly what is is that you're supposed to know about it. For example, most students will only say or think something like *Learn the parts of the cell*, when in biology. That's not specific!

You should think something like *Learn the location, function, and the makeup of the plasma membrane, the cytoplasm, the ribosomes, and the DNA*. This should be your goal! Always go for depth, because the better you know, the more you know.

By being more specific, you are communicating to your brain what it needs to learn, and it responds without you even knowing it. It starts processing the information in the background, kind of like your phone downloading a song while you're snapchatting or texting. Your brain starts to make new connections and look for information it already has on these topics. You will also pay more attention to the specifics you specified when you read, listen to, and watch stuff about them.

Being specific is going for understanding. Many students just skim the surface and never really learn, because they just fill their minds with general unconnected nonsense they quickly forget.

The thing is that your future depends on how quickly you can learn and how well you understand and apply the information you're learning, not on how well you can repeat and forget it. You dig?

Go deep. Always.

Chapter Summary

To avoid procrastinating on big projects or tests, create specific goals and plans you can follow. This will prevent mental overload your brain evolved to defend itself from. When using specific goals and language, you help your brain focus on, find, understand, and use the information you're learning better. Better is good. Bad is not.

Specific your learning must be, before learn it you can. - Yoda

Chapter 4: Use the Right Method

What you'll learn

Every subject requires a unique learning approach. It's best to figure out how to learn something before you learn it. There'll be examples!

Use the Right Method

I often see chemistry students trying to memorize chemistry definitions. This approach might work for a vocab quiz. But what if I change how these definitions are worded? The words mean the same thing, but are different. Psych! I don't mean to be evil, but I want my students to understand concepts. I want them to be able to figure things out.

I hope you have teachers who do that too, because if they just feed you information and ask you to repeat it, they are setting you up for a future full of disappointments. It's because no matter what you end up doing for work, you'll have to be able to figure things out; and not just to solve problems, but also come up with creative solutions. And you just can't learn this by repeating what some book says.

To solve a problem, you need to understand the problem first, often from multiple perspectives, and then you must know how to begin solving it. You need the right approach.

There's a method to this madness they say, because the approach you choose has to fit the problem you face. Same goes for learning. It makes little sense to approach learning chemistry the same way you study history, right? It might seem obvious, but I see students try and fail to apply what works in one class to another all the time.

It doesn't work. Always ask yourself: *What am I learning and what's the best way to learn it?* If you don't know, ask your teacher what she recommends or just google *the best way to study _____.*

I don't want to leave you hanging here, so I'll give you some subject specific examples.

You can study random words in **Spanish**, but if you're going on a Mexico trip, you're better off knowing basic phrases such as *Hello, Thank you,* and *Where's the bathroom 'cause I really need to go?*

If you're learning **chemistry**, say solving **stoichiometry** problems, write down the steps your teacher, book, ot the web gives first. Then, look at example problems and learn to identify each step. It's key to understand what each step actually does, so think about it. Next, solve problems on your own, identifying each step and knowing where you are in the process. You can start by solving problems and looking at examples as you do it. The end goal is to get to the point where you understand the steps and can do them on your own.

Learning **math** or **physics** is similar to stoichiometry. You might have a fewer or more steps and formulas to use, but you always want to understand what you're doing. Mindless repetition is for zombies.

If it's science, business, or social studies **concepts** you need to master, the best strategy is to use them somehow. You might explain how mitosis works in your own words to a younger sibling or create a business plan for your future ice cream joint. Drawing a comic and using it to explain a historical event or recording a video comparing and contrasting US and Canada will help you remember these things better than reading and rereading text about them.

Need to change your **car's oil**? YouTube. Pop the hood. Crawl under.

And now the obvious, but not so obvious, and super useful hack.

Humans have one really stupid expectation of themselves: *We expect to know something before we even learn it. (?!?!)*

I do it all the time. Looking back, I could have saved a lot of time and frustration by being smarter and asking others questions. So... If you are having trouble figuring something out on your own, get used to asking for help. Most people are happy to help. They welcome questions, because it lets them shine. Experts want to use their know how. Otherwise, what's the point of having knowledge and skills?

Problem is we're not asking. We just go it alone. Dumb, isn't it?

In a perfect school, teachers would teach the important stuff; the things you can use and care about right now. I'll admit that a lot of stuff I teach in chemistry is useless. There are things though, that might help in the future. Which ones? I'd tell you if I knew.

I hope education is heading in the direction of teaching more of the things you want to learn and fewer of the noise variety, but in the meantime, you can learn how to figure everything out.

Chapter Summary

The point is that if you learn how to figure out the best method to learn a concept or skill, you'll become a quicker learner, but getting this process going may be slow and frustrating at first. Each subject is different and requires its own approach. Sometimes the tweaks are small and sometimes huge. The struggle is real, but if you have the chops for it, you will come out on top.

Jedi who knows the way, strong is the force with him. - Yoda

CHAPTER 5: BE OPEN-MINDED

What you'll learn

How open or how closed you are to something affects how your brain deals with it. *Are there things you do to prevent your learning?*

Be Open-minded

Sounds simple enough, doesn't it? Except, students do things that prevent them from learning all the time. They sabotage it by sending conscious and unconscious messages to their brain that say *Don't learn this!*

I caught myself doing this only recently. I signed up for this summer work program for teachers with a big company to make a buck on the side. The people leading the program warned me that the learning would be intense, but the truth is that I set myself up to fail before it even started. I never gave myself a chance.

You see, summer is my writing time, but my family needed money for a down payment on a new and bigger car, so in opposition to my gut, I signed up. In the weeks leading up to the start date, I kept thinking how I would adjust to the corporate world. I even planned on writing a blog series titled *Corporate Slavery*, on the trials and tribulations I encounter during this experience.

See what I did there? I had a negative connotation for the whole thing before it even began! I also kept thinking about all the things I'm gonna hate about it and how it will take time away from writing. I wondered how the rigid, and I didn't even know if it was going to be rigid, work and schedule will kill my summer. Then I started.

During my first and only week in the program that normally lasts six weeks, I was bothered by the busy work, the 2 hour law and statistics lectures I was supposed to bring bag lunch to, and the unexciting lab work. I am a quick learner, but I was overwhelmed with all the new information I was learning and exhausted at the end of each day.

But the truth is that there were 30+ other teachers in the program, most of whom I am sure were enjoying it and learning as a result. I didn't. I mean, I learned a few things, but by being close-minded I made learning a lot harder. And then I did the best thing I could have done, next to never signing up for the program. I quit!

So what's that got to do with you?

Being in a class you don't like sucks. If it's not a requirement, ask for a different placement. But if you have no choice but to be there, the best course of action is to first accept it and then find things you can like about it. Maybe the teacher is okay. Maybe you get to hang out and learn with a friend. It might also be fun to get to know another student. Whatever it is, you have to start steering your mind toward a more positive place. If you don't, you won't learn.

Whether you are aware of it or not, your brain listens to all the messages you send it and is very good at ignoring things that are not important or ones that overwhelm you. It throws them out. So, even if you're trying to pay attention in a class you hate, the negative feelings toward it prevent you from remembering and understanding the material. It sucks to be in there, but if you're always negative, you won't learn much and you're unlikely to be successful.

And that's just one part of it, because if you're negative, you won't be able to pay attention and fully engage in the learning to begin with. You will hold back. Something will always drag you down.

And there's more...

In the previous chapter, I mentioned our really stupid tendency to expect to know something before we learn it. That holds us back too.

Though it seems like a no-brainer that the whole idea of going to school is to learn, I see students beat themselves up all the time when they don't know the stuff I'm about to teach them before I teach it. I catch myself doing it as well. I bet you sometimes do it too.

Do you sometimes feel *not as smart* when learning something new around people who know more than you about it? I'm talking about situations in which you should just allow yourself to accept that you don't know it, relax, and listen with an open mind so you can learn. If you do that, you will know it soon enough.

The real problem happens when you try to mask it; hide it somehow. It prevents you from engaging and asking questions. What's worse, such behavior slows down, even stops your learning.

Chapter Summary

So allow yourself not to know everything. When you do, you will learn more. You will also be more successful if you look for the positive aspects of things you generally dislike, because you want to communicate to your brain that though school and life get hard sometimes, you're ready to go *beast mode* on them.

Your mind open you must. Beast mode reach you will. - Yoda

Chapter 6: Practice Smart

What you'll learn

Do you read and reread your notes or textbook when studying for a test? What else are you doing? If you said many things, that's good, because the more you do, the more you learn. You gotta do different things and engage all your senses. If it ain't smart, it ain't that good.

How to Practice Smart

You're not an actor trying to memorize your lines for the school play. I love and go to school plays all the time, but learning is not an act. It's a journey, and because learning is more complicated than a play, you need to do it the smart way. The awesome thing is, that if you learn the smart way, learning itself will become much easier.

Smart practice, smart learning really, is about 3 things: *active learning, smart repetition, and mixing it up.*

Active learning is about engaging as many senses as possible and application of knowledge and skills during learning. If you've ever been told that you are a visual learner, you've been lied to. You are NOT. You DON'T learn best by hearing, or reading, or doing either. Sorry if I burst your bubble here, but I want you to crush school, so I must tell you that despite of what you might have been told in the past, you learn best by doing ALL of those things.

That's right; you learn best by using not one particular, but all of your senses. The more, the better. There are many studies that support that, but instead of boring you to death, I ask that you ask yourself this: *Have you ever met anyone whose brain is exactly the same as your brain?* Even identical twins process stuff differently.

So, if you prefer learning by watching videos, watch videos. But don't just watch videos. Read about the topic you're learning, take notes on it when you can, recall information from memory, explain it to a classmate, draw a diagram about it, or record your own video on it.

Some other things you can do with information are paraphrasing, summarizing, comparing and contrasting, writing skit scripts, making graphics, building models, and talking about what it all means. The world is your oyster. Just remember: *The more you do, the more you learn.*

Smart repetition involves recall; the constructive struggle to find the information buried in your brain, as opposed to repeating formulas and definitions mindlessly.

This is important, because as a teacher I see my students doing it wrong all the time. Many think *reviewing* is about doing something along the lines of *reading the book and reading the notes over and over until they throw up, fall asleep, or die.*

Okay, that last one is extreme, but extreme circumstances call for extreme measures. If you're at least a little guilty of doing some variant of the above, it is time to level up your learning. Do it by using *recall.*

Instead of reading and rereading, practice explaining the concepts from memory. It's okay to use the book or notes for help at first, but you want to get to the point where you can comfortably explain the concept, without any help and using your own language.

Make your mind struggle. Force it to find the information. Read over the concepts if you can't, then try it. Look at the third concept on the list and talk about it. Do it with other concepts. It will sink in. When? That depends on the amount of info and number of repetitions.

Mixing it up means alternating between learning of different concepts and skills and using different learning strategies. It works, because though you like your routines, doing things differently and giving your brain a fresh look at stuff, helps you understand and remember concepts better.

So what does that actually look like when you study?

First, don't just repeat one concept 10 times and move onto the next. Rather, practice it for a while, move on to the new concept, then another, and then come back to the original concept. If there are 5 concepts you need to study, alternate. This pattern could look something like this:

1 *2 3* 4 5, **1** *3* 5 *3* 4, *2 3* 4 *1* 2, **1** *2* 4 5 *3* etc. Get the idea?

The pattern is what you decide it to be, but make sure you jump between different concepts or problems several times, so you feel confident no matter how they're thrown your way.

Second, use many study strategies. If you're asking why, because what you do now kinda-sorta works, you probably weren't paying attention to my learning styles story earlier.

Okay, I'll spare you, but close your eyes and imagine if Sir Caveman only used sight and ignored his other senses. If he ignored hearing, do you think he'd be able to ignore the pain that follows a sabre tooth cat digging its 12 inch fangs into his back and chomping on his flesh? Fast forward to today and you're eating roadkill and dumpster diving is a highly paid profession. All because smell is overrated.

So whether you're learning in class or studying at home. Mix up the way you use the information you're learning.

Hack time. Don't blink 'cause it'll be quick. *The best way to learn something is to teach it.* The more opportunities you have to explain something to someone else, the more expert you become at it. Fact.

Chapter Summary

You can practice hard, but it won't be effective if you don't practice smart. **Learn actively** by engaging all your senses when studying. Use **recall**, which is *smart repetition*, as opposed to mindless repetition that leads to gross and/or dangerous outcomes. And don't forget to **mix it up**, because alternating what you're learning and using a variety of ways to learn, is where learning's at homie.

> *Mindless repetition to the dark side leads. Not using recall to not learning leads. Not learning to frustration leads. Frustration sucks.*
> - Yoda

CHAPTER 7: SPACE PRACTICE OUT

What you'll learn

Cramming just ain't the way and you need to know why so you stop doing it. Let me show you the easy brain science way to spend the same amount of time studying with much awesomer results.

Use Spaced Practice

Remember what you had for breakfast on Wednesday 2 weeks ago? If you do, you're either a genius or you need to diversify your breakfast menu. Just sayin'.

The point is that unless you remind yourself about what you had for breakfast on Wednesday 2 weeks ago every day, several times a day, you just won't remember. It's pretty useless information to begin with, and unless that day was somehow special, your brain says *meh* and throws it out.

Information needs to sit in the brain and be recalled several times for it to stick. Say you're one of those people who likes the same bowl of Cheerios or Froot Loops to start off their day with every day. I'm not judging; just pointing out that you actually do know what you had for breakfast on Wednesday 2 weeks ago, because your breakfast routine repeats a lot. You take it for granted, because it's normal, but your brain actually gets spaced practice and that's why it remembers.

Learning is the same way. Your brain stores things it is using at the moment in its working memory. If the information isn't used, your brain throws it out. This is why you, and everybody else on this planet, forget pretty much everything you learn. Bummer, I know.

So unless you meet a highly advanced alien who can teach you a way to store everything you want in your brain soon, you need to figure out how to get information to move into your long term memory.

How do you make sure stuff ends up in your long term memory? Here's a simple example. If you have a test coming up on Friday, you could study for 5 hours straight the night before. Unfortunately, much of this crammed information will not stay in your long term memory.

But, if you can find it in your heart to study for an hour each day, or can fit in ten study sessions into 5 days, say 30 minutes each morning and evening, you would have spent the same amount of time studying.

The magical thing that happens though is that by allowing the information to sit and your brain to form and strengthen connections, the concepts are now in your long term memory.

You see, many students make the mistake of thinking that remembering and understanding is about *how much you study*. It is not. True learning; the kind that results in you being able to recall and apply the knowledge and skills you learn, is about *how much you study, how often you practice*, and the *time in-between the study sessions*.

But it isn't just about remembering and storing information. Spaced practice is key to understanding. For the hard stuff to sink in, the brain must alternate between the focused and the relaxed mode. It needs smart spaced out practice and frequent breaks for neural connections to become stronger and to form new neural connections that lead to the formation of meaning.

The basics of this process of meaning formation or understanding are the same for everyone. What is different is the amount of time and the number of repetitions it takes. But, as often in life, this is something you must figure out for yourself, because it is your brain and it's unique. And that's a good thing.

Hopefully, you have teachers who let you figure out concepts and practice problems in class. Hopefully, they come back to the information and have you use it multiple times over several days or weeks. But if they don't, you now know what you have to do on your own. Better yet, get a few friends together and do it as a group.

How about a vocab quiz hack that can be used for tests too? Say you have to study for a 30 term vocab quiz. Here's the hacker's way:

1. Create smaller categories by grouping most closely related words together.
2. Study 1 to 3 of those categories at a time.
3. Break to stand up, stretch etc. if you start getting tired.
4. Mix it up (Chapter 6) and repeat over several days.

Chapter Summary

Learning is like playing sports. If you only practice the night before, chances are you'll suck. Your team will suck too. The fans will be witness to a suckfest of a game; all because of you. But if you practice often and don't give up, you and everyone else will have a lot of fun. You won't always win, but you will feel proud and have respect, because you held your own.

Spaced practice you must use. Or suck you will. - Yoda

CHAPTER 8: FOCUS ON THE PROCESS

What you'll learn

Ask your future self: *Was getting that A in English more important than being able to write and communicate my ideas really well?* Ideally, both are true for you 10 years from now, but I want to show you how to focus on learning and why it leads to success that lasts.

Focus on the Process

Education is evil. Not learning; the educational system is rigged. It's set up to counteract its very purpose, because as messed up as these things are, schools often pay more attention to grades and scores than to what you actually learned. GPA, ACT and SAT, honor roll, National Honor Society; those things matter for college admission, but the rest of the world doesn't care. Not really.

The world of work that you'll enter sooner than you think, is opposite. The bosses want to know what you know and what skills you can offer. They care about the ways you fit their vision and how you can make their companies better. High school GPA? Not so much. And if you decide you want to work for yourself? I've never seen an entrepreneur claim National Honor Society membership on their resume or LinkedIn profile. Do they even need a resume?

In the meantime, parents are slapping straight A student stickers on their bumpers and no one bothers to ask what skills their kids have. That's messed up and it's a societal problem. Chances are, you've been programmed by the world you live in to focus on grades. I'm not saying they're not important, but if you stop and think hard about it... *Doesn't it seem like there's something really wrong here?!*

Okay. let me get off my soapbox before I pop a vein. Learning is more important than grades. Skills are more crucial to success than test scores. Being able to communicate, collaborate, and create in the global society is way more important than National Honor Society.

Why is it that many game changers, people who shape our world in the most profound ways, are college dropouts? Steve Jobs. Dropout. Anthony Hopkins. Oscar winning actor with ADD. Richard Branson. Dyslexic Billionaire. Bill Gates. Nerdy Dropout. Even Warren Buffett, the oracle of Omaha, a brilliant mind who invests and makes billions with scary consistency, was rejected by Harvard.

These are just a few examples of people whose encounters with formal education were less than perfect. But they have three things in common; they're rich, they love learning, and they didn't let traditional schooling interfere with their learning. In fact, they never stopped learning.

Your brain does what you tell it to do. If you focus on grades it will look for the easiest way to get grades, which often prevents learning.

So, if you've been infected with this disease, start reframing. Work on shifting your mindset from a grade focus to a learning focus. If you decide to constantly improve yourself, success will come as a result. You might not always get the best grades, but I suspect you will get good grades, and I know you will set yourself up for future successes. High school lasts 4 years. You need to think *life*.

I'm not promising you'll become a millionaire, but I know for a fact that if you don't learn, your life will suck. Luckily, it's never too late to start. It's never too late to change. I was stuck in one place, not really doing much more than my nine to five till I was 37. And then I took an online _Learning How to Learn_ class and my life changed profoundly. Now, I make it a point to learn something every day.

What I'm asking of you is hard. When the amount of information you need to learn seems too much, you get overwhelmed, you start procrastinating, and you worry about grades all over again. Everyone experiences this at times. The best way to deal is to chunk.

Chunking might seem like an obvious thing to do, but it is a Jedi mind trick of sorts. When you plan things out (studying for a big test or completing a huge project) on paper and you physically separate the tasks you have to do, your brain starts to relax.

Say you have 20 big concepts to learn for a final. Here's your hack:

1. Write down all the topics.
2. Group the most similar or related topics into categories (chunks). Keep each chunk small; 3 to 4 topics is magic.
3. Write out which chunk you will study when. Be specific about the dates and times.
4. Mix it up, use spaced repetition and recall.

I guarantee the test won't feel as big after you put your plan down. Take a big breath. Now exhale. Now work your plan and crush it.

Chapter Summary

You don't need to look at the top when climbing a mountain. Just draw a map, focus on going in the right direction, and don't trip. When school or life overwhelm, chunk and focus on getting each part done one by one. Never stop learning. Get skills. That's not just a school thing. That's a good life thing.

Grades not make one great. Skillful a Jedi must be. - Yoda

Chapter 9: Singletask

What you'll learn

You've heard why you shouldn't multitask a million times, so I'll tell you what *singletasking* is all about. I'll make it quick and give you a little hack that will make a huge difference.

Singletask

When learning something, focus on learning alone. This is hard. All the usual distractions are there. *How do you prevent them and focus on one thing only? How do you singletask?*

Enter *pomodoro*.

Huh?

The Pomodoro Hack

Pomodoro is a 25 minute chunk of time that can be used to do deep focused work. Like studying. Here's how you Get. It. Done!

1. Have a specific task in mind, or better yet, write it down.
2. Set the timer on your phone or watch to 25 minutes.
3. Kill the distractions. Phone? Airplane mode. Desk? Clear. Door? Closed. Fam and friends? Informed. You? Game.
4. Focus on and do the one task alone till the timer sounds.
5. Take a 3 to 5 minute break.
6. You can do a series of pomodoros as needed. Just remember to take breaks and restart the timer each time.

Why should I do some weirdly-named dumb thing, if I can just focus and study?, might you ask.

The answer lies in this unrecognizable thing; an edge that pomodoro gives your brain. Following the steps of setting a specific goal and a 25 minute deadline, and being deliberate about killing distractions, allows you to achieve *laser focus*. You communicate to your mind, body, and spirit that this is what you need them all to do. All your thoughts, emotions, and body parts work in unison toward the same singular purpose. This synchronicity of your whole being crushes it.

Don't believe me? Try it! I guarantee, you will get more work done in 25 minutes that you ever thought possible. More than you've ever done. But don't thank me. I'm just the messenger. You're the one in the trenches. It's all you.

You decided. You're about to crush it.

Chapter Summary

Use the pomodoro strategy when studying or working on a project and you will achieve insane productivity.

Multitasking clouds everything. Learning well impossible is.
- Yoda

Chapter 10: Prioritize

What you'll learn

Which details are the most important to understanding the big idea? What is the big idea? Can you always answer these questions when learning something new? Do you know how much time to devote to each task when working on a project? Do you plan it out? When you know how to prioritize, learning is less frustrating. It becomes easier.

Prioritize

Prioritizing is rarely taught in high school. Often, teachers expect you to have learned it in middle school, and if you don't speak up, they never find out. Then, you get lost and confused. This leads to frustration, because although you have the ability to understand what they're teaching, you lack the needed prior skills or knowledge.

For example, teachers might assume you know how to take good notes, which is mainly about picking out the important information and choosing what to write down. You might copy word for word, fearing you'll omit important information. You get all the info.

Problem with this approach is that you're not prioritizing the important stuff; the concepts that are key to understanding the main objectives of the lesson. As a result, you can't make connections between information taught now and in the past.. There seems to be no relevance either. The learning is shallow. It sucks.

How do you do it better? For one, make sure you read and write down the learning objectives each day. If your teacher skips this part, ask about what the big ideas to know from today are. When taking notes, write down the information that supports these main ideas.

Secondly, it is absolutely crucial that you know how to take good notes. Many students don't like taking notes, because they find them useless. Most of the time, the reason for this is that they write too much and don't know how to pick out the important stuff. They don't know how to prioritize.

The best way is to learn note taking in school. Ask a teacher or a friend who knows and uses a good system to show you. You can also go online and pick and stick with a system. I use a special version of Cornell notes. It's my _Cornell Notes on Steroids Notebook_.

You should also prioritize, when completing big projects. It will help you avoid procrastination and frustration. Planning the project out in advance is the best way. What's really cool about this, is that it's very similar to making a study plan, which you've seen in <u>Chapter 3</u>. Here's your last hack, the

Prioritize That Project Plan

1. **Write down the big tasks and put them in order.** If you're writing a 5 paragraph paper, this might look something like (1) Sources, (2) Outline, (3) Intro, (4) Body 1, (5) Body 2, (6) Body 3, and (7) Conclusion.
2. **Take each big task and add and order smaller tasks.** This could be (1) Research Online, (2) Go to the Library, and (3) Use the Textbook; for your sources section. You can also list the ideas to use in your Intro or each Body paragraph.
3. **Focus and do one task at a time.** Do one big task at a time e.g. once you have your Sources and Outline, you can write each paragraph of your paper based on your listed ideas.
4. **You don't have to finish in one day.** Relax, you planned it.
5. **Polish it up.** Once the project is completed, review it to make sure everything makes sense and flows. On papers, make sure you connect paragraphs using transitions.

Prioritizing helps learning and project completion, because it helps your mind focus on the most important topics or tasks. As a result, you remember and understand better and your productivity improves. Your mind holds the 1 to 3 main tasks/concepts in your working (now) memory and finds details and examples that add to their meaning as you learn, study, or work on a project.

Frustration occurs when you don't know how to prioritize info and your mind gets overwhelmed perceiving it as *too much*, when all you need is a trick or two to make it more doable.

Chapter Summary

Because your mind forgets or ignores most information it receives, you need to learn to prioritize. Learn to prioritize important info while studying and plan projects out, so you can avoid frustration that causes procrastination. When you prioritize, you remember more of the stuff you're supposed to learn. Then, you learn.

Prioritize what you do. Save you it can. - Yoda

Conclusion

I hope you enjoyed the 10 Secrets and learned a lot, but I have to be honest with you: *The 10 Secrets aren't really secrets.* They are truths. Some are universally known, in which case they're not so secret. Others are often hidden.

What is often unknown is why exactly these secrets or tips work; the brain science involved. I hope this book provided those answers.

What is obscured is how these things impact your understanding and memory. I hope this book helped with that.

Often, these learning tips become secrets by being skipped over or brushed aside in favor of teaching curriculum; the chemistry, the geography, the math. You are told to study *it*, but often not given the right tools to study *it*. I hope this books gave you those tools in the form of skills you can use for the rest of your life. Not school. Life.

Because learning; *knowing how to learn*, is the one skill that you can use and will need to change the world.

Change your world first.

Then decide how far you want to take it.

Always remember, and never let anyone tell you otherwise:

You have the power to change the world.

I hope you use it often.

Thanks to...

My wife and son: Thank you for being part of my life every day and accepting me as I come. You inspire me to be a better husband and father every day. I love you.

Sean: Thank you *Mr. Future US Senator from New Jersey* for always encouraging me, believing in me, and giving it to me like it is, real. Go get them in 2018! #OurFutureFirst #BrothersForever

Jon: Thank you for inspiring me and helping me be a better human and writer. Keep killing it on My BAD! #BrothersForever

Bam Radio Network: Thank you for continued opportunities and support. I look forward to the podcast and promise to kill it.

Rob: Thank you for being my partner in crime. Let's Keep Ed Real!

Family & Friends: Thank you for being there when I need you; wherever you may be...

PLN, you know who you are: Thank you for support and always pushing me to be a better educator and person. I think it's working.

You: Thank you for reading. Please text/call 651.757.6635 or email me at oskar@focus2achieve.com if you have any questions. Really.

You have my gratitude, love, and respect. I look forward to continuing to earn my keep.

Crush School 3...

Made in United States
Cleveland, OH
05 June 2025

17499416R00024